GW01066273

Managing Children's Behaviour

A practical guide for nursery professionals

Ruth Andreski and Sarah Nicholls

A

publication

About The Authors

Ruth Andreski is an adviser on early years education. She is known nationally as a writer and a speaker on the subject.

Sarah Nicholls was a University lecturer (early years) at Reading University. She is currently lecturing privately and writing on educational matters.

Acknowledgements

We would like to thank the following people for their help and support in writing the book:
Pauline Hansford for word processing the script.

Childbase Nurseries, their managers and staff for valuable observations.

Our family and friends with whom we can "bounce around" ideas.

Published By Nursery World Limited ©1997
Production Manager: Gary Smith Production Assistant: John Thompson
Managing Children's Behaviour **is available from Nursery World Ltd,**
Lector Court, 151-153 Farringdon Road, London EC1R 3AD
(sales hotline- 0171 837 8515)
Origination & Printing By Valiant Printers Ltd

Contents

INTRODUCTION

This book is written mainly for professionals in 'educare' settings. Interested parents may also find it useful when judging such settings or in their dealings with their own children. We use the term nursery to include all pre-school establishments. It is not a book about 'crisis scenarios', where everybody is at their wits' ends, though we have devoted one chapter to such situations. We have chosen to take a broad view in relation to managing children's behaviour and believe in the old adage that prevention is better than cure. To this end we have spent some time looking at possible underlying causes for troublesome behaviour. Without an understanding of these it is difficult, if not impossible, to rectify, or at least improve, matters.

The very long period of infant and childhood dependency necessitates a good deal of self sacrifice and altruism on the part of carers. This, and the fact that humans need to co-operate in almost all they do, demonstrates that elements of 'goodness' are very much part of our innate character. Unfortunately, we also have the propensity to be selfish and are capable of all sorts of nasty things in order to satisfy our appetites and desires. Our success as educators in helping to get the balance right is of crucial importance, not just for society, but also for individual happiness.

Psychology has taught us how the treatment of the very young influences, to a large extent, their view of themselves and their attitudes to others. In writing this book we have drawn not only from our knowledge of current theory, but above all, on our own experiences after lifelong work in the education of young children. Our case study materials are born out of this experience. We give particular attention to the crucial role of parents in developing children's emotional wellbeing. A chapter is devoted to them.

We have also considered the importance of the adult's role in interacting with children, creating the right environment and planning those parts of the curriculum

4

which are primarily concerned with the expression of feelings and the development of a sense of responsibility. In addition, we know that many settings use television/video and all use literature as part of their educational programme. We have suggested ways of making best use of the potential of these for influencing attitudes and behaviour.

We recognise children's need for a consistent framework for discipline, and to this end present a Behaviour Policy for discussion and consideration by professional groups and parents. This policy focuses upon positive rather than negative rules.

Finally, we hope readers will find the book free of unnecessary jargon and that it will help them, in a practical way, to tackle this area of major concern.

CHAPTER ONE

The National Picture

Every time a new and shocking revelation about children's behaviour hits the headlines both politicians and public thrash about to find explanations and answers. There is no shortage of scapegoats identified by the great and the good among us, who pontificate from their safe and often distant position. In the meantime, experienced practitioners working with young children and their families feel a certain sense of unease. It has become increasingly obvious to them that the way our society rears its children is failing for a variety of reasons. They have observed, at first hand, a change for the worse in children's behaviour. Indeed an overwhelming number of respondents to our questionnaire[1] agreed that behaviour had deteriorated over the past ten years.

Moreover, professionals in childcare and education find that increasing demands are made of them to the extent that they are often asked to try to compensate for poor parenting and, at worst, repair damage caused by neglect or abuse. We set out below some of the factors which we think are responsible for this state of affairs:-

THE CHANGING NATURE OF FAMILY AND COMMUNITY

To say that there ever was a 'golden age' for family life is probably unrealistic. However, there has been a very clear shift from the time when a family almost invariably consisted of two parents and their children, supported by a network of relatives and neighbours of long standing. Communities were much more stable in the past, people tended to work close to home and were less mobile, and the breadwinner often did the same job for a lifetime. Change occurred much more slowly, and a certain sense of security could be gained from the orderliness in a community where everyone knew everyone else and roles and relationships, customs and beliefs were more clearly defined and more universally shared.

Today we live in a time of rapid social change brought about in large measure by the information technology revolution. The nature of work has altered for many people and there is greater insecurity. This has been a major factor in breaking up the extended family into nuclear units, often living at some distance from each other and therefore unable to offer the example and support available in former times. These changes have put pressure on families. Parents who find that marriage does not live up to their expectations seek a way out through divorce, so that now nearly a quarter of families with dependent children have only one parent - in 90% of cases this is the mother. Such changes have clearly been hard on children because not only do they suffer the 'loss' of a parent, their financial situation deteriorates too and the remaining parent bears the pressure of doing the work of two. A staggering 2.3 million children in this country now lives with a single parent in this situation[2].

If the separation of parents is acrimonious then the children suffer even more by acting as pawns in a particularly nasty game. When this happens the father, for it is almost always the father, is frequently absent from the scene. With this change will probably go grandma and grandpa and the aunts and uncles from his side of the family as well. Another worrying feature of this situation is the fact that when parents remarry, children are required to make difficult emotional adjustments to a new web of relationships. Today, one in twelve children lives in a step family.

THE CHANGING SITUATION FOR MEN AND WOMEN AT WORK

Generally speaking, women today are better educated and have much higher career expectations than their predecessors. Seeking success in their own right is no doubt in part due to their perception of the insecurity of marriage as a career and the cult of individuality which has characterised the past twenty years or so. Moreover, the nature of jobs today frequently favours women over men. 66% of mothers now work, albeit some part time. The dual role of motherhood and career is demanding, particularly in high powered jobs. Inevitably there must be less time for children and certainly a lot less of that unhurried time to listen and share experiences. Perhaps this has played a part in the increase in referrals of children to child guidance clinics. Indeed, as a recent research study conducted by the

West Berkshire Health Authority and Reading University's Psychology Department has shown, problems with young children are spread right across the social spectrum[3].

It would be unfair, however, just to blame the absence of mum from the scene. Today's father is required to work such long hours, often even sacrificing weekends, that he can almost become a stranger in his own home. The cult of the 'workaholic' may seem to make sense to the business community, but we disagree. Short term gain may appear advantageous to a company, but the long term consequences of employing stressed and burnt-out parents will be grave. After all, tomorrow's workforce depends upon the children of today growing into well adjusted future citizens. Secure emotional bonding between children and parents needs time spent together, and a recent Mintel survey revealed 20% of parents admitting to NO PLEASURE from time with their children[4].

CHANGES IN PARENTAL ATTITUDES TO CHILDREN'S FREEDOM

Today's parents are very apprehensive about letting their children out on their own, even though the statistics show that there are no more child murders and abductions now than there were 25 years ago when 80% of seven- and eight-year-olds walked to school unaccompanied by an adult. By 1990 only 9% were doing so. In a recent survey nearly half the parents questioned said they never, or hardly ever, let their children play out without adult supervision. This caution is as much to do with the density of traffic, with its inherent dangers, as it is with the fear of madmen (or women)[5].

The downside of this fear is, of course, that many challenges and opportunities, such as pitting their wits against the forces of nature, problem solving and sorting out relationships for themselves, are denied to children. Because few adults are willing to accompany them out of doors for as long as they would like, or need, the result is often confinement.

Confinement has a number of undesirable consequences for children. They are unlikely to be able to develop bodily functions such as circulation and respiration to their full capacity, with important negative consequences for their health in later life.

Confinement is also likely to build up a kind of frustration which can only be

8

released through vigorous physical activity, popularly known as 'letting off steam'. How many so-called hyperactive individuals are really only very energetic children who need to run about outside until they are tired!

And it is not just children's physical development that is likely to be impaired through keeping them indoors too much. According to a recent newspaper article, Dr Ned Mueller, a clinical psychologist, claims that confinement can retard intellectual development as well. In another article, Dr Elizabeth Newsome of Nottingham University says that children are not learning independence and the ability to 'rough it'. She maintains that there is a greater sense of achievement to be had from battling with the elements than winning a computer game[6].

A CHANGE IN TOY CULTURE

Clearly parents are faced with a problem. If their children cannot be allowed to play outside, they need to be kept occupied in the home, and this has led to a considerable change in the toy culture. Between 1991 and 1995 there has been a 49% increase in the sales of electronic games, and millions of pounds are spent each year on them. Furthermore, nearly half of seven- to ten-year-olds have a TV set in their bedrooms (Central Statistical Office).

The change in the toy culture is also manifest in a Euromonitor study which highlights a shift away from outdoor communal pursuits to indoor solitary ones. There has been a 12.5% fall in UK sales of equipment such as swings and climbing frames between 1991 and 1995. Admittedly this was a time of economic recession, but faced with the choice, parents clearly preferred to spend on toys to occupy their child's mind indoors rather than his whole being outside!

CHANGES IN OUR DEMANDS OF CHILDREN

There is certainly an insidious pressure upon children to grow up, rushing them out of each natural developmental stage into the next. They are presented at an increasingly early age with images of fashion, dining out (they even have their parties at hamburger restaurants now), needing to look attractive and so on. The former teenage culture has crept lower and lower down the age groups so that now it is to be found in the infant school. This hurry to false maturity is heavily promoted by advertisers who know full well the power of offspring to cajole their parents into spending money. There is no financial gain for them in children's 'carefree time' spent making mud pies, catching tiddlers or creating home-made camps in trees.

Another very important pressure is placed upon our children in Britain as a result of such an early start in formal education. We are, as far as we can ascertain, the only country in the world where formal education starts at the age of five. This means that many children are being asked to do things for which they are not yet ready developmentally. A formal start to learning too soon leads to considerable numbers of our children - particularly boys - deciding that education is not for them. Early failure and dissatisfaction is built into the system.

International tables of comparison do not support our practice. Those who enter school at six or seven, and who have had longer in a nursery setting, actually do better. Furthermore, it is our bottom 40% who present most cause for concern in relation to academic achievement, and it is those children who suffer most from such early demands. National Curriculum testing at seven helps to pile on this pressure.

Finally, a consequence of the recent political desire to provide for all four-year-olds in some form of education is that many were absorbed into unsuitable settings. A child who is only just four is not helped by being placed in an understaffed and overcrowded classroom where individual needs cannot possibly be catered for.

CHANGES IN THE DISTRIBUTION OF INCOMES

During the past 20 or so years British society has become increasingly polarised so that the rich became richer and the poor poorer. Today, according to a Barnardos study, one in four children live in poverty. While the poor have always been with us, they have never been so exposed to the realities of inequality.

Advertising and the media make children aware of the multiplicity of goods on offer to those who can afford them. It is the job of the advertiser to generate a desire for the material goods he presents. If this desire is frustrated, as in the case of the children of the poor, it will probably lead to a sense of injustice. The 'it's not fair, why can't I have those things?' mentality frequently leads to anti-social attitudes which can, in turn, form the basis for bad behaviour.

CHAPTER TWO

An Enabling Environment

It is important to construct an environment that is supportive of children's development as this in itself will avoid many of the frustrations that lead to bad behaviour. Elements of this frustration have been outlined in chapter one, particularly the issue of confinement, and we must compensate as far as we are able by providing a child-centred facility which will enable their social, emotional, physical and intellectual needs to be met.

We should aim to provide 'can do' situations in 'can do' surroundings. Therefore the elements that need to be at the forefront of our planning are Time, Space, Resources, People and the Rules which bind them together in harmony.

TIME

If we want to produce children who are capable of exercising such skills as forward planning, implementation (carrying through tasks), concentrating and persevering, it is clearly essential that they must be given blocks of uninterrupted time to pursue their own goals.

However, it is obvious that no social setting can function without certain time constraints, even if they are only the beginning and end of each whole session/day. What must be addressed is the question of balance between necessary and unnecessary routines, where the latter may only be for staff convenience or through force of habit.

Let us assume that uninterrupted blocks of time have been identified. These do

11

have to come to an end. It is essential that endings are prepared for sensitively through staged warnings, for example. three minutes, two minutes, one minute to clearing-up time. Such a warning has the advantage of being objective and begins to provide the children with an understanding of the concept of the passage of time. This will also help them with their personal planning.

SPACE

A child's environment should neither be over- nor under-stimulating, and both indoor and outdoor facilities must be considered. A setting which fails to use the outdoors for a considerable part of each day is not meeting all the children's needs nor compensating for the confinement they suffer elsewhere.

FEATURES THAT NEED TO BE CONSIDERED ARE:

Outside:

Safety and security
Physical challenge
Intellectual challenge
Social interaction
Natural world
Man-made aspects
Storage
Opportunities for exploration and discovery
Creative and imaginative outlets
Quiet places for observation and reflection
Variety of levels and surfaces
Pathways
Area markings to facilitate individual and group games
Areas of sun and shade
Gardening, harvesting and habitat
Use of the wider environment including buildings, people, work, transport, parks, gardens etc.

Inside:
•All the features listed above, except for the last four, equally apply to the inside. However, specific consideration should be given to:
•The relationship of one activity to another, for example book corners need to be away from noisy activities
•Sound absorbing materials to promote a quieter working space more conducive

12

to purposeful play
•Display areas both vertical and horizontal to exhibit items to stimulate and satisfy curiosity and contributions from children to promote their self-esteem.

RESOURCES

A 'can do' environment which fosters independence requires resources (which can be used safely) to be accessible to the children without recourse to adult permission. This means that storage furniture could be labelled commensurate with children's ages and stages. For example, a box of Lego should have a piece of Lego, the picture and the word on the outside for easy recognition.

Resources which are displayed such as water play equipment can benefit from a background silhouette for immediate identification and matching.

Many smaller items such as paintbrushes and pencils can be openly displayed in suitable containers for ease of access.

Items of clothing both personal and communal should be hung on hooks/pegs at the right level for the children and labelled.

Giving this freedom of access to the children also involves giving some responsibility for maintaining the resources, both for themselves and others. A simple code of 'Get it, Use it, Return it' promotes personal and social responsibility.

PEOPLE

All the people connected with a setting - employees, visitors and friends - need to be aware of their responsibility as role models. So manners, speech, body language, willingness to help, dress, care and consideration are all important.

Adults are there to:

•Support children in achieving individual goals
•Devise activities to educate them
•Maintain the quality and safety of the environment

13

•Establish and maintain a framework for acceptable behaviour.

This leads us on to the question of establishing appropriate and well understood rules which embody personal conduct, care and respect for others/creatures, and responsibility for property/environment. A more detailed look at rules is provided in chapter 5 on creating and implementing a behaviour policy.

CHAPTER THREE

An Expressive Curriculum

In chapter two an enabling environment was discussed in which children can explore their surroundings and have time and space to come to terms with their own personalities and development. Within this environment it is essential that professionals provide a broad and balanced curriculum. However, in relation to children's behaviour and their social and emotional development it is even more vital that the aesthetic, creative and physical sides of their natures are allowed full range and exploration. This will enable them to begin to understand and develop their own self-control and self-awareness, and that should in turn lead to happy, balanced young individuals.

What is an expressive curriculum? It is the elements of learning that feed the imagination, wonderment and physical expression of the wide range of human feelings from deepest sorrow to great joy, from the isolation of the individual to the effective group member. How do we provide for the development of these emotions? Let us look at areas within young children's experience.

ART

There are many expressive media that can be used in art, but two of the most common and flexible are painting and modelling.

Painting - The most usual image of painting that comes to mind is water paints and a brush on paper. This is very valuable and allows children freedom to portray significant images in colours they choose. It gives them some control over what they have seen or heard by putting images on paper that determine the size and importance of living beings or inanimate objects in their lives. Children may then wish to speak about their paintings or not, and here the adult should show

15

empathy and not insist 'tell me about your painting'. Painting can be explored further if adults provide the children with a variety of paints, brushes, implements, paper, card, wood and other materials to paint upon, and put these either in the vertical or horizontal planes. Through adding to the experience of painting, adults will also provide children with a wider vocabulary to express themselves and turn it into a collaborative experience. Painting can also be ephemeral or more permanent as in finger painting. Here, children can absorb themselves in pattern and picture making, having total control over whether they keep their images by printing them off or rubbing them out. This gives children the power to be in control in a very calm situation.

Modelling - There are a variety of media that can be used for modelling, such as dough, Plasticene, playdough, natural materials (sand, earth, wood) and, most importantly, clay. Clay has certain elements that are invaluable in learning to understand change, to be in control of change, and also to understand that materials can be indestructible in one form but fragile in another. All these experiences can be gained from working with this material, enabling children to express anger by banging the soft clay, being in control when modelling their images, changing the images as they model and then, in the drying or firing of clay, making the images permanent. Then they learn that these models have to be cared for as the material is now breakable.

Both in painting and modelling, children must learn to care for the equipment. Then others can use it, share the materials and look after themselves and the environment, keeping as clean as is sensible in the circumstances. Adults must allow children to make a mess and explore fully what they are doing, but equally the responsibility for clearing up the mess must be part of the whole experience.

MUSIC

Music can be exciting, frightening, lively, happy, sad, slow, or fast. There are probably as many words to express music as there are emotions. We do not have to be musicians to experience those feelings. What we must provide for children, though, is a variety of music to reflect the emotions and the opportunity to express themselves through making music or moving in response to it. Here the important element is a wide range both in mood, type and tradition. If we provide children with unlimited background music of, say, Radio One or taped examples they begin not to 'hear' it and fail to respond in any way except by ignoring it. This is not healthy for their emotional or even intellectual development. Music should be chosen wisely and played for a purpose and children helped to discriminate

16

between rhythm, pitch and volume. They should also be encouraged to respond to what they hear, learning to use music as a creative outlet for their own feelings.

Their response can be to join in through song or rhythm, to sit/lie still and listen, to move freely or experience the discipline of a dance pattern. Whatever it may be, while responding to this creative element in human development they may relax and 'lose themselves' to the music or develop a sense of group identity through dance or song. Such experiences form an essential basis for children's creativity in music-making. For this to develop further a wide variety of both commercial and home-made musical instruments must be available. From simply making sounds to telling stories to their music patterning, children can express their deepest feelings.

PHYSICAL

Expression through physical movement has been touched on in response to music, but it is important that children have every opportunity to be physical in response to their emotions in our increasingly sedentary lives. Not only do they need to be physical, but they need to learn how to control their bodily responses to anger, pleasure, fear, excitement and so on. For this to occur there should be provision that is both structured and unstructured. Through dance and drama led by an adult, children can be helped to control their bodies, express moods, work individually or in groups, travel through a storyline to a conclusion or follow their own imaginations, and develop their language. Children also need outside space that is safe but challenging, to let off steam, explore their physical capabilities, learn to mix in small or larger groups and share the resources co-operatively. Without this opportunity to be free, we cannot expect children to adjust to the quieter more controlled responses to emotions and turn these into creativity.

NATURAL WORLD

It is important that children can experience and respond to the natural world and see themselves as part of the continuity of life. They need to have living things to care and take responsibility for and to realise that without their attention domestic animals and plants could die. In turn they will come to see how people need to care for themselves and others. Working outside through digging, planting, tending and harvesting food will also teach them patience and a sense of success as a result of their labours. Gradually, they will learn to defer gratification.

ROLE PLAY AND STORIES

Role play usually takes place in some kind of home corner, and is valuable in enabling children to re-create and come to terms with their own home circumstances. However, the corner can also be changed into many different environments, such as an office, station or hospital, and children develop their understanding of adult roles and life around them through play in these areas. Using their imagination in these settings, the children create relationships and learn to work co-operatively. Role play can also occur outside on a much larger scale, when climbing frames become 'buildings', or bushes become a den. It is vital that adults allow children the space and time to create their own characters in these circumstances but be on hand to help when necessary. This help may be in the form of arbitration, addition or subtraction of materials or provision of further knowledge through discussion.

The following scenario depicts co-operation and negotiating skills as the adult hands over responsibility for conflict resolution to the children, through skilful intervention and discussion:-
Setting - role play
Dispute - who has the crown
Actors - two four-year-old girls and one adult.

X snatches crown from Y's head - 'That's mine. I want to be Queen' (tears follow).

Adult: 'So you both want to be the queen, but we only have one crown - What can we do?'
Y: 'But it's mine - I had it first'.
X: 'Yes, but I want one'.

Adult: (insistently) 'But we only have one crown. We have to do something so you can both enjoy the game.'
Y: 'We could make another one with that gold card'.
Adult: 'What a good idea - I'll help you'.

Role play often develops naturally into children's own stories, allowing them to verbalise what they have experienced so that they and others can understand the sequence of events. For children to be able to do this, they must have been exposed to a variety of literature by adults providing the language for them to talk about all sorts of experiences, and understand the pattern of storytelling.

The stories must be both imaginative and true-to-life, reflecting all the emotions and social situations that they may meet.

SMALL WORLD PLAY

This is another most valuable means of the child projecting his/her imagination on to symbolic items representing real world entities. It may be played by a solitary child or by a group. It gives children the valuable experience of 'being in charge', playing out emotions, understanding symbolism, developing a story-line and thus verbalising the actions they control.

CHAPTER FOUR

Developing a Sense of Responsibility

Achievement on the part of a child is personally satisfying, but perhaps even more important it earns, or should earn, adult approval and adult praise. Such acclaim builds a child's self-confidence and self-esteem, and a feeling of emotional well-being, all of which are necessary conditions for happiness and all of which are highly co-related to positive social attitudes and good behaviour. They produce an 'I can do' mentality which is psychologically healthy and conforms with the innate desire of the young to assume independence and responsibility.

The experience of early adult praise and support seems even more important for boys than it is for girls. Their egos appear to be more fragile and they are more easily discouraged by initial failure. They will tend to reject those things they are failing at, preferring instead to seek peer acclaim by challenging authority, acting the fool, talking tough or behaving aggressively.

In order to guide children towards success, adults should use their knowledge and expertise to judge the amount of time allowed for free choice within a safe and organised environment. Choice itself demands a measure of responsibility. Those who are always told what to do and are denied the right to decide for themselves are likely to lack initiative, independence and judgement. They can, at worst, become dangerously compliant to authority. Moreover, selfset goals are normally within the capacity of the individual to achieve. When one considers that the environment within which the child operates has itself been controlled by the

20

adults, who should have faith in their judgement, then whatever the child chooses ought to be profitable. Children's time should be balanced between being directed and choosing for themselves.

HOW TO SUPPORT CHILDREN IN ACHIEVING GOALS, WHETHER SELF-SET OR ADULT-DESIGNED

Children should be encouraged to think about the sphere in which they wish to achieve. More lengthy or complicated activities need planning. Adults should make reference to planning in relation to an organised activity: stating the aim and sequence of events and pointing out materials and equipment that will be used. They should also support individual children by helping them through discussion to define:

- What outcome is required?
- What materials/equipment are needed?
- Where are these to be found?
- Where will the activity be carried out?
- Any pre-activity requirements? For example, putting on an apron - a likely sequence of events with relevant 'what if' questions.
- What to do after completion of the activity?
- Should tangible results be displayed, stored, recorded in some way?
- Tidying up.

Such discussions help a child envisage, sequence logically, and consider problems before they happen (and perhaps avoid them). Importantly, they demonstrate adult interest and support. There should be a review at the end. Discussions like this also do much to develop language which empowers the child to use his/her intellect rather than resort to an undesirable aggressive response born of frustration when things go wrong.

Children who have learned to behave responsibly will undoubtedly get more out of their education and are likely to enjoy relationships and their work much more than those who have not. The adult remit here is of very great importance.

It goes without saying that all acts which reflect a sense of responsibility should be the subject of generous praise.

We can divide the nature of responsibility into four categories:
1. Responsibility for self

Children need to assume responsibility for themselves as individuals. There are a variety of ways in which this can be done:

•Personal hygiene - children should wash their hands before meals or cooking activities and after going to the toilet or handling things which could possibly carry bacteria.

•Children should be made aware of and increasingly assume responsibility for putting on aprons when engaging in painting, water play or cooking.

•They should know the place for personal belongings such as coats and shoe bags and use these properly.

•It is important that during parts of the day they should be free to determine for themselves what activities they undertake and be encouraged to evaluate what they have done.

•They should clear up for themselves after activities.

2 Responsibility for the environment
It is never too soon to encourage children to take responsibility for features of the environment, within their competence. Here are some of the things that can form part of their remit:

• Recognising that living things brought into the nursery or nursery garden are entirely dependent on them for their welfare. To this end, they should take part in housing, feeding, watering and the careful handling of animals, as well as cultivating plants.

• Sometimes choosing the theme and furnishings in the home corner.

• Locating, using and returning items to their rightful place.

• Helping to prepare for activities by, for example, paint mixing or covering tables before craft activities.

• Contributing ideas for and helping mount displays.

• Creating and maintaining habitats for creatures in the nursery garden.

• Encouraging and caring for wild birds.

• Using the litter baskets.

• Helping to maintain resources in good order.

3. Responsibility for others

Let us consider different activities which involve responsibility for others. At this stage in children's development 'others' might include dolls and toys which they imbue with human characteristics. Such activities might include:

• Caring roles in the home corner - parenting, providing medical treatment, veterinary treatment, looking after visitors.

• Comforting other children or toys in an imaginary situation who may be upset or have hurt themselves.

• Making items for the pleasure of other people - Mother's/Father's day cards, little gifts for people who have helped us, presents for friends etc.

• Helping people relay verbal or written messages from one part of the nursery to another.

• Telephoning (real or imagined) people who may not be well on any given day and asking how they are.

• Dictating or 'writing' letters of comfort or pleasure to people.

• Dictating or 'writing' thank you letters.

• Talking at group time about people who help us.

• Discussing characters in stories who have shown kindness to others.

• Using 'need narratives' - stories where a need is identified and where children discuss how they can meet that need. Such a story may be about a teddy bear who has travelled from France and has lost his way. He is very cold, very tired and very hungry. When the children have suggested how they can help him with all these needs they can then think of ways he could get home.

Of course the successful outcome of this activity will depend on the skill of the storyteller and her subsequent presentation of need, willingness to consider all the children's suggestions and creation of opportunities for them to actually make things to help the bear!

4. Shared responsibility
Here it is important that each child plays his/her part in order to achieve the common goal. We give, as an example, an activity which is likely to take place in all settings - snack time.
What is described is well within children's competence and offers a first class opportunity for all members of the group to see the importance of their own role for a successful and enjoyable outcome.

PREPARING FOR SNACK TIME

By dividing the task up into discrete units, in what can be called 'a system', members of the group assume their essential role. Each unit is printed on to a card with an illustration to symbolise what is entailed. The cards are then laminated to protect them and placed in a 'preparing for snack time' tin. Children choose these, lucky dip fashion. The units could be:

1.The cloth. Select one from the drawer and lay it on the table. At the end of snack time, brush off any crumbs. If the cloth is clean it can be used again. Fold it up and put it away in the drawer.

2.The table decoration. You can choose the table decoration. Do you want flowers? Or you can choose a decoration from the drawer and bring it to the table. When snack time is finished clear the decoration away.

3.The invitations. Take the name cards and invite all the people in your group to come and sit at the table.

4.The drink. Collect the two jugs of drink and bring them to the table. Now collect as many mugs as you need. Ask everybody what they would like and pour out the drinks they choose. Clear away the mugs and jugs at the end.

5.The snack. Prepare the fruit and toast on two plates. Have two kinds of fruit and two kinds of spread on the toast. Make sure there is a plate for everyone. Hand round the snacks to the group asking people what they would like. Clear away the plates at the end.

Of course, before introducing such a system, the adult will have to talk through what each card is asking the children to do. With daily use it will not be long before the children can 'read' the instructions for themselves.

The advantages of such an organisation are:
1. It involves no favouritism on the part of the adults.

2. Everybody gets to have a go at everything over time.

3. The group will appreciate that the pleasurable outcomes of snack time depend on individuals sharing responsibilities.

4. The activity is part of the 'real world of work' at an appropriate level. Such 'real' experiences are too often denied children nowadays.

5. If adults involve themselves skilfully in this task then every single one of the six areas of children's learning will be covered to some degree.

CHAPTER FIVE

Creating and Implementing a Behaviour Policy

A workable behaviour policy should have the following underlying features:

•It was created by all the adults concerned with the children.

•It is realistic in its demands - based on a sound understanding of child development.

•It is understood by all concerned - staff, parents, visitors and students.

•It is communicated effectively to the child/ren.

•It is implemented consistently and fairly.

•It affords opportunities for children to exercise some choice within the defined framework.

•It is regularly reviewed.

•It is capable of recognising that individual children will learn to conform to its expectations at different rates based upon their nature, experience, and cultural background.

The policy itself must be explicit and based upon the following rules:

26

A. Not hurting others.
B. Not saying unkind things.
C. Not taking or damaging other people's property.
D. Not harming any features of the environment, particularly living things.
E. Not offending others through bad manners.

We believe, however, that any behaviour policy is likely to be more effective if it is based upon a positive viewpoint and focuses upon actions and behaviour we wish to instill. Let's turn the rules around to read more positively.
A. We always try to be kind to others.
B. We always try to speak nicely to one another.
C. We look after our own and other people's things.
D. We take care of our home/nursery.
E. We put things back where they belong.
F. We look after living things.

These positive statements are few in number and easily understood. Too many rules confuse and often lead to nagging, which is counter-productive. When a child transgresses, we condemn the behaviour not the child.

THE BEHAVIOUR POLICY

The following embraces all the principles professionals need to consider when writing and implementing a behaviour policy. It is essential to remember, however, that every setting will need to form their own with their specific needs in mind: the process of team discussion provides underlying understanding and a sense of ownership and as a result it should ensure consistency in application.

Example policy (You might discuss this as a basis for creating your own).
We recognise the individuality of all our children.
We work in partnership with the children's families.
All adults concerned with the children accept their responsibility for implementing the goals enshrined in the policy.
The policy recognises and will implement the Code of Practice for children with special educational needs when appropriate.
This policy will be regularly reviewed to ensure that any new knowledge will be considered and new circumstances catered for.
There are four basic principles/rules involved:
A. We look after ourselves (safety and welfare).
B. We care for others (avoiding actions which might hurt either physically or

27

emotionally).

C. We all recognise our responsibility in relation to the natural and man-made world around us.

D. We respect other people's property and their constructive activities.

THESE PRINCIPLES, AS COMMUNICATED TO ADULTS, ARE PRESENTED TO THE CHILDREN IN THE FOLLOWING WAYS:

A. We do not run indoors.
   We wash our hands before handling food.
   We wash our hands after going to the toilet.
   We clean our teeth after meals.

B. We don't hurt other people.
   We don't say and do unkind things.
   We don't throw things (except in ball games).
   We don't push and shove.
   We share things and take turns.

C. We look after our animals and plants.
   We put things back when we have finished with them.
   We try not to break things.
   We tidy up after ourselves.

D. We do not take things which do not belong to us.
   We do not spoil other people's games.
   We do not spoil other people's things.

It is important to remember that your own actions and behaviour in relation to these principles will communicate their message more strongly than your words. However, it is essential that you explain, comment upon, praise or admonish when necessary. In this way both your actions and words will be mutually re-enforcing and enable children to begin to internalise a moral code.

Parents must of course be shown this policy, have it explained if necessary, and could be asked to sign a contract of agreement that they will support it in action.

CHAPTER SIX

Parents in Partnership

We cannot consider children's behaviour in isolation: it is inextricably linked to their family circumstances, both influenced by them and influencing them. Indeed, parents and children are just as much the cause of each other's problems as they are of each other's joys.

Childcare/education professionals are frequently asked for advice and support from parents who, without example from other family members, are often left feeling isolated and confused by the unrelenting demands of their infants. Although some may be 'whizz kids' in information technology or high finance, they can feel at a loss to know what to do with an infant's non-compliance with what they see as quite reasonable requests! Such parents are used to things running smoothly, to being in control of situations and to the kind of predictability which usually goes with efficient organisations.

Other parents find their task daunting for quite different reasons. They may be facing the stresses of financial difficulties, job insecurity or depression. Life for such people is difficult enough without the added burden that parenthood places upon them. There are also some parents who have not had the benefit of good parenting themselves and therefore have little idea of how to interact or play with their children.

The interface between the professional and parents needs to be characterised by trust and understanding. It is important for the former to proffer any advice and support with extreme sensitivity and to remind themselves that, unlike parents:

29

• They have received, or are receiving, training for the work they do.

• They work in a child-centred environment with lots of toys, planned activities, materials and equipment which holds special appeal to children and where they can express themselves freely.

• Staff have clearly defined hours of work and can go home at the end of the day - unlike parents who have ultimate responsibility for their offspring 24 hours a day, seven days a week for at least 18 years!

• Professionals work in teams so that there is lots of 'colleague support'.

There are a number of ways in which support can be given to parents without seeming to preach. Success is more likely if we generate confidence and encourage people to trust their own instincts, judgement and common sense. We should help to demystify childrearing. After all, humanity has come this far reasonably successfully! So, what can we do to help those who look to us?

1. We can encourage them to come into our settings, see what sort of things we give children to do: water, cardboard boxes, digging in the earth, rolling out pastry and so on all engage children's attention. They are not expensive and busy little people are much less likely to be naughty.

We show how we are relaxed with children, how we discuss things with them and offer choice and freedom within a framework of discipline.

2. We can organise a parent's group which meets regularly and at suitable times. For those who do not work this will probably best be when their children are actually in the setting, during the day. For working parents evenings may be the best time. In such groups parents are likely to derive much benefit from simply talking to others in the same boat. Whether they choose to focus their discussion on a particular topic or whether discussion naturally ensues round other activities (fund raising for example) should be a matter for them. Some groups may welcome the inclusion of professionals who may be able to join in informally.

3. Professionals might put on a session for parents devoted to a particular topic of their choice relating to children's behaviour. Such a meeting could include a talk from an invited speaker, with opportunities for questions afterwards or having a panel to whom parents can address particular concerns. In either case it is always

a good idea if parents write down their questions in advance and hand them in anonymously because:

A. The questions can be shared out and answered by the best person.
B. Parents have had time to think of the most pressing question facing them and phrase it in the most appropriate and effective way.
C. You avoid possible embarrassing silences and situations where parents would like to ask questions but don't dare in case they sound 'silly'.

4. Another possible scenario is to set up regular discussion sessions run by the manager and/or staff members on particular topics which typically worry parents. These may include:

temper tantrums   aggression towards siblings
bedtimes   jealousy
confrontations/failure to obey
meal times/eating
being rude to other people, perhaps using bad language.

5. You can work with parents to set up a joint behaviour policy to ensure consistency between all the significant adults in a child's life.

Such a session might begin by the setting presenting its behaviour policy for consultation and review. Then it can go on to emphasise the need for consistency and how this helps the child's moral development.

It may be helpful to present the following points to parents for their consideration and discussion.
- Children need praise and feel loved when they receive it.
- They do not like criticism, it is isolating and unpleasant.
- Over time they learn which actions are praised and which are criticised.
- The child absorbs this information and translates it into his own ethical framework.
- You can often tell when this is beginning to happen by his reactions to the behaviour of friends in a real life situation. In play you may hear his judgements expressed on the 'behaviour' of dolls, toys or even the family pets!
- This ethical framework is internalised and becomes an individual's

conscience. It is a kind of internal policeman forbidding some actions which are potentially pleasurable and commanding that others be done out of a sense of obligation.

• Internal policemen are, of course, much more effective in controlling behaviour than other forms of discipline. A well-balanced individual needs a 'policeman' who is neither so strict as to create anxiety nor too permissive!

•Looking back at the first two statements it must be clear to everybody that it is a lot easier to sort out an ethical framework if all the adults in a child's life praise and criticise the same actions.

Groups of parents might then like to consider the following views about discipline generally.

VIEW A

'Children need a clearly defined framework of what is and what is not acceptable. We need to explain clearly why we ask them to do or not do certain things. We should expect them to conform - in a kindly way of course - and if they transgress then they should be appropriately punished.'

VIEW B

'It's best not to be always moaning. Children should be allowed to do what they want within reason. If you're too strict and inflexible then you'll end up with timorous little mice with no guts or initiative - you know, the sort of people who follow authority blindly.'

Ideas for discussion about specific issues, for example bedtime.

VIEW A

'Bedtime should be a set routine. It should be at the same time every night, preceded by a bath or wash and tooth cleaning. Then the parents should read the child a story, kiss him/her goodnight and then lights out. That's the end of the story. Parents need a little bit of time to themselves to relax and do what they want to do.'

VIEW B

'It's just not worth having arguments over such trivial matters as bedtime. Children will want to go to bed when they are tired, then there's no hassle which is bad for both the parents and the child.'

Common sense points to add here:
•Plenty of fresh air and physical exercise are good for children and will make them tired and more likely to sleep!

•Try not to have too many rules. Decide what really matters to you and stick to it. Give children some choices within the general rule, eg 'Would you like me to read 'The Three Bears' or 'Little Red Riding Hood' when you go to bed?'

We have been talking so far about settings working with their parent body on general issues of children's behaviour. Now we need to look at the way professionals and parents can work together on a more intimate one to one basis.

As part of general good practice there should be an easy, informal relationship whereby either party can raise issues of concern at any time. In addition to this both should be adding their observations to a child's record and this record should include a heading - Personal and Social Development (SCAA Nursery Education Desirable Outcomes For Children's Learning on entering compulsory education, January 1996).

Criteria against which personal and social development are judged are:
    1. Have confidence and self respect.
    2. Behave in appropriate ways.
    3. Be aware of right and wrong.
    4. Work well in groups and be willing to take turns and share fairly.
    5. Treat living things, property and their environment with care and concern.
    6. Have good relationships with and sensitivity to others, including those of different cultures and beliefs.
    7.Show a range of feelings such as wonder, joy or sorrow.
    8. Respond to cultural and religious events.
    9. Concentrate and persevere.
    10.Take initiative.
    11. Be able to select an activity or resources.

33

12. Work well independently.
13. Have personal independence (eg in dressing, hygiene).

These recorded observations should be the subject of formal discussion and ways ahead sought so that children's development in this area can proceed satisfactorily.

In some cases the observations of either or both parties may highlight causes for concern with regard to children's behaviour. Such causes for concern, if they stem from psychological or often more physiologically-based conditions will constitute the first stage of a special educational needs procedure and should be entered on your SEN register. Put the emphasis on the concerns that are in the child's interest and add any information parents have which may throw light on a condition, eg general health or traumatic circumstances, which will be helpful in building up a general picture.

You can then work together keeping detailed observations under the following suggested format:

Observation

Name: D.O.B

Date	Day of week	Time	Others Present	Situation	Observed Behaviour

It may be that the observations you are both keeping highlight a pattern and even a causal link with bad behaviour. If so, action can be taken to avoid the triggering circumstances. In any case such observation will form a very useful basis for discussion with any other professionals who may need to become involved in the future.

At this stage you will meet regularly to review progress and if, after two such reviews, the child's behaviour has improved you may, with luck, find that the child no longer has a special educational need and that all is now well. However, you should keep the child's name on your register until you are certain that this is the case. If there has been no improvement in the situation, or it has worsened you may feel that you need to move to Stage II. You will work closely with parents again and advise them that you intend to draw up an Individual Education Plan for

34

their child to help him/her. You will also, together, need to gather all the information you can from other agencies: Social Services and/or Health may be involved and ask parents for any advice which their GP may have to offer. It is possible that there are social services concerns about the child's welfare and in very serious cases the child may be on the Child Protection Register. The local authority may be responsible for him/her under the terms of the Children's Act. The setting responsible for the care/ education of the child may need additional help through for example, a pre-school special needs counsellor, an educational psychologist or a health visitor. Contrive to hold regular reviews with the child's parents at least once every 12 or so weeks. If no progress is being made then the whole procedure goes a stage further to bring in an outside specialist. This is likely to be an educational psychologist, and he or she will make a formal assessment of the child's needs.

At all times you will be working closely with parents and putting any advice received from other specialists into practice. Again you will be meeting regularly with them to review progress. Good progress may mean that the child can revert to stage 2. It is not likely that pre-school settings will deal with stages 4 or 5. In the case of 5 a legally binding statement of Special Educational Needs is issued and provision to meet these needs must be made.

Further helpful information on procedures for SEN is available free from the Department for Education and Employment. They will send you a book, *Special Educational Needs Code of Practice*, if you phone in your request on 0171 - 510 - 0150. The circular No.9.94 'The Education of Children with Educational and Behavioural Difficulties' is also obtainable free from the same department.

35

CHAPTER SEVEN

Some Cultural Influences on Children's Behaviour - Acceptance or Control?

We have discussed elsewhere how home, nursery and the relationship between the two are the paramount influences on children's behaviour. In this chapter we shall be looking at other factors which affect it and which tend to assume increasing importance as the child grows older.

As in so many spheres of human activity, the handwringing, tut-tutting concern of bystanders seldom achieves much and can even be responsible for the very things they deplore. What we are advocating is that adults play a more active role in controlling certain cultural influences. These will differ in type and intensity according to individual circumstances. We have chosen to focus on those most likely to affect everybody in an educare environment and over which we can probably exercise a considerable measure of control. They are:
- Television/video.
- Literature.
- Cultural climate (ethos and resources).

What can we do in relation to the above?:
Assess the degree of their impact in our own setting.
Control them ourselves and do our best to ensure that others will do the same in order to maximise their positive side.
Be knowledgeable about them. This will probably mean pre-viewing television programmes while video recording them. It will mean running through software

36

programmes before purchasing/using them, pre-reading the literature you intend to present, and being very selective before buying toys, games, equipment etc.

TELEVISION/VIDEO

The great advantage of recording television programmes is that you can then watch them and judge their suitability in terms of their moral messages and quality of language. It also means that you can think about how you will use a programme. You might choose, in front of very small children, to make a comment like, 'Wasn't that kind of so and so to act in that way?' or, 'That's not a very nice thing to do.' With slightly more mature children you might ask them to make judgements for themselves - 'How did the little boy help his Grandma in the story?' ... or 'How do you think the little girl felt when the birds helped her?' You will also have time to devise valuable follow-up activities which balance the rather passive nature of television watching.

The moving picture holds great fascination for children. It seems to have an almost hypnotic effect on them. Used judiciously, it undoubtedly has great educational value in that it can expose children to environments, cultures, natural phenomena and so on which are normally outside their experience. The sheer range of television coverage has the potential to expand horizons. It may also be useful in increasing children's vocabulary and may expose them to good language modelling. It can explain difficult concepts, often through the use of skilful graphics (this is particularly possible in good computer software). Of course we must not forget the value of television in simply providing enjoyment.

Like so many wonderful things, though, it does have its downside. First, children can become too passive if they watch it a lot. It is one-way communication responsible for all the talking and all the action. Inactivity leaves the abundant energy of young children unspent. This is made worse if the action portrayed causes a flow of unused adrenaline!

A second negative feature of television is its tendency to flit relentlessly from one item to another. A child watching cannot stop it, ask it questions or change in any way what is happening. The rapid transfer from scene to scene - advertisements here, cartoon characters there and documentary material somewhere else, together with the 'zapper' button offering yet more incoherence, is likely to impede children's powers of concentration. Excessive viewing, remote control in hand, often promotes sensation seeking and programmes which do not satisfy this demand may be ignored - encouraging inattentiveness generally. Some professionals in speech therapy and health visiting have noted how the television is never switched off in some homes and blame this among other factors for the increasing numbers of children with speech and language problems.

Dr Sally Ward, an expert in children's speech and language and a respected therapist, has conducted her own research. She has recorded how, whereas over ten years ago the number of children with difficulties was 20%, it is now nearing 40%. Dr Ward's research is pointing the finger at the constant background noise of television. Where this is present adults often do not talk to their children and teach them nursery rhymes and songs. Thus children are not gaining the experience of listening. Without such experience they have difficulty in distinguishing significant foreground from unimportant background noise. All this makes the later study of phonics, so important in learning to read, very difficult indeed.

The frequent portrayal of violence or anti-social behaviour is another worrying feature and forms part of an ongoing debate about TV's role in promoting violence in our society. Research evidence is, at present, rather inconclusive on this issue. However, of the people questioned in a recent Nursery World survey on children's behaviour, the overwhelming majority (98%) of respondents working in nurseries felt that television characters influenced behaviour. Many TV characters behave violently. Interestingly, the research carried out by Lefkowitz et. al. (1997) found that boys appear to be more influenced by television violence than girls. Whether this is because boys tend to be more aggressive anyway and therefore want to watch such programmes or whether the violent programmes make the boys aggressive is a difficult question to answer[7].

We believe that violence shown on the screen is much more likely to affect children if it reinforces what they are experiencing already in their life. Moreover, a diet of violence without adult guidance may have the harmful effect of desensitising children so that they are neither shocked by it nor capable of empathising with the victim.

Advertisers certainly recognise the power of the medium to persuade the young to purchase their products! If it influences purchasing behaviour, why not other kinds?

We have talked about controlling rather than passive acceptance of what's on offer. Aware of the potential positive and negative influences of the medium, we should act upon our knowledge.

What can we do? Well, give careful consideration to the following points which should prove useful in putting you in charge:

Control the time allowed for watching.

Balance the passivity of television with active, creative, and expressive work. If a programme has stimulated such work then it has been valuable.

Exercise your critical judgement about a programme - could its message have been better conveyed in a first-hand mode? For example, why watch bead threading or birds feeding when you can actually thread beads or set up your own bird table? Could you present the message better yourselves?

Allow plenty of time for discussion. Encourage the children to adopt a critical approach to what they are offered. Did they like the programme? Then go into a number of appropriate open-ended questions about it to expand this judgement. Focus particularly on the sayings and doings of the characters in relation to good or bad behaviour. Encourage children to empathise.

Another very important topic for discussion is whether what is happening is real or fantasy. Small children are often confused over this and muddle the two. Without the guidance of a loving adult to help them sort it out, much fantasy (and often violent) material may be considered 'real' and therefore present the world as a much more violent place than it really is. A child may come to believe that violence and aggression are behaviour one should adopt in order to 'fit in'.

THE IMPORTANCE OF THE LANGUAGE MODEL

Mastery of language increases a child's capacity to think about her actions and their consequences. It therefore aids self-control and encourages communication by words rather than (often violent) actions. Understanding and using language effectively is essential for educational success and so, indirectly, it is tied up with self-esteem. Moreover, behaviour management is helped if we can encourage children to think (for which they usually need language) about their actions and the possible consequences of them. Impulsiveness is a characteristic of the very young so, in effect, we are seeking ways of helping children put language between an initial impulse and the action that follows. But how can we set about doing this?

• By presenting good language modelling ourselves, speaking clearly and grammatically correctly. When introducing new words we recognise that context will help children to understand their meaning, but we cannot be sure of this. It is therefore important to check for understanding and explain if necessary.

• By offering a rich diet of literature.

• By encouraging discussion which will involve children in all the main uses of language: making statements, asking questions and issuing commands. They should talk about past and present events and predict happenings in the future.

• By inviting people into our setting to talk to children about any number of things from commentaries on the kittens they have brought in to their collection of shells to their hobby of playing the flute!

• By affording plenty of time for purposeful play. This in itself generates some of the most valuable opportunities for using language. It is one of the main justifications for play featuring so prominently in early years education.

Mention must be made of the importance of listening in all this. Many professionals complain that children find it increasingly difficult to listen these days. One reason for this is undoubtedly the cacophony of noise that fills their environment. However, if they cannot and do not listen, children are excluded from receiving information presented to them through the aural sense. They miss out on vital language modelling and we cannot be sure that they have understood our explanations and injunctions in relation to the behaviour we require. So, as well as doing all of the above to develop language we also need to consider the environment in which language is taking place. Noisy and quiet activities should be separated because discussions and story sessions need to take place in tranquil surroundings.

THE CULTURAL CLIMATE AND ITS INFLUENCE ON CHILDREN'S BEHAVIOUR

We must all be aware of just how important the early years are when shaping children's attitudes. For this reason great emphasis is placed by the regulatory authorities, backed up by legislation, on offering a programme of learning which includes other people's cultures and beliefs. If this did not occur then ensuing ignorance and prejudice can all too early lead to unacceptable behaviour by both groups and individuals.

There are three main reasons why practitioners must get the cultural climate right. One, through helping children acquire knowledge and understanding about other people, and their culture and religion, and showing that diversity can be both interesting and enriching, we promote tolerance. Tolerance is far more likely to lead to decent behaviour than narrow-minded views which often condemn others.

Two, it helps counteract the tendency all groups have to believe that they and their way of life are superior - and by implication that others are inferior. Three, it helps children to feel in harmony with society. They belong because they see their group and its culture represented and sometimes even celebrated.

If we turn the situation round and look at the likely consequences of not getting the cultural climate right, we must be struck by the serious nature of the responsibility placed upon us. Intolerance and prejudice so easily leads to ugly bullying behaviour including name calling and physical abuse. Victims feel a smouldering sense of injustice which translates into either withdrawal or combative behaviour.

Feelings of exclusion, as well as damaging an individual's self-image, may also lead to anti-social behaviour. Imagine wanting to paint a picture of your mum and there being no colour or possibility of mixing one that matches her skin tone. Imagine if, among all the images and artefacts around, you could not see anything that relates to the way you look or the things you do. Wouldn't you feel alienated? Indeed, you might even reject such an unpleasant society together with the education it is trying to impart. Is your establishment confident about the measures it employs to promote good behaviour and social harmony among different ethnic groups and a sense of well-being among individuals?

Do you, for example:
• Celebrate diversity with tastings and feastings of other cultures' food?
• Go through your books, artefacts, pictures etc to make sure that they portray and represent varied cultures and beliefs?
• Enable children to try on other people's style of dress, play with their kind of cookery utensils and put their kind of dolls to be in the home corner?
• Tell stories from varied cultures?
• Encourage empathy through discussing issues such as belonging and exclusion?
• Play music from a variety of cultures?
• Encourage children from different cultural backgrounds to co-operate in pairs and small groups?
• Invite representative adults to visit your setting and tell children about the way they do things?

THE IMPORTANT INFLUENCE OF TRADITIONAL LITERATURE

Modern literature has much to offer in terms of freshness and immediate relevance to children's lives. However, it is imperative that they be exposed to the wealth of traditional literature in the form of fables, folk and fairy tales because:
• These provide a common cultural heritage which contributes to social cohesion.
• They include characters which clearly embody either good or evil (small children cannot cope with shades of grey in this regard).
• They present situations where good triumphs over evil.

41

•They do not present an immediate solution to the challenge. In identifying with the characters, children are led to understand that perseverance in the face of dangers and difficulties ultimately succeeds.

•The modern tendency of protecting children from the unpleasant and frightening can be counter-productive. By meeting such dangers through literature children will acquire strategies to recognise and cope with them as and when they occur in real life.

•Children will learn that time must often elapse before goals can be reached.

•Actions, guided by the moral tenet of good winning over evil, will determine 'happy endings'. These in turn present the future in a positive light.

•Exposure to such stories helps to build an individual's moral code in preparation for adulthood.

•Regular exposure to such stories should help provide children with the emotional security to cope with their own fears.

CHAPTER EIGHT

Underlying Causes of Abnormal Behaviour

It is important to distinguish between mildly troublesome behaviour, which all children display from time to time, and its more extreme and persistent form. The former may have a variety of causes ranging from tiredness and hunger to the child simply being off colour.

In this chapter we shall explore some of the underlying causes of behaviour which disturbs the harmonious working of the nursery or the home. One must recognise that many of the causes of difficult behaviour lie outside the nursery, having their origins in the child's family circumstances. Indeed sometimes staff in a nursery may find themselves involved in these circumstances, perhaps being asked for help or advice by the child's parents. In more extreme circumstances, they may be asked to provide evidence before a court if child abuse is suspected.

EXPECTATIONS

Children may behave badly in response to unrealistic expectations on the part of those who care for them. Such expectations may take one of two forms. The first reflects a lack of understanding on the part of an adult about children's normal development. They do not appreciate that all small children are essentially egocentric and that they cannot, at this stage, be rightfully accused of being 'spoilt', 'selfish', 'bad mannered' etc. Such an adult may expect a child to be 'good', and be able to control his emotions, and when such expectations are not met they may resort to harsh verbal or even physical punishments.

43

'**James is over two now. Whenever I take him to the shops he shows me up. When I'm standing talking to my friends he keeps interrupting and pulling my arm for me to get him an ice cream or whatever. If I ask him to wait a minute he only shouts and has a temper tantrum. I often end up smacking his legs. He should be able to do as he's told by now.**'
Frustrated mother

Another form of unrealistic expectation relates to intellectual achievement. Over-ambitious parents may want to use their children to reflect glory upon themselves, to be a form of status symbol. Sometimes this can become a group phenomenon where different sets of parents vie with each other to see whose child is making the greatest progress in for example literacy or mathematics. Such expectations are harmful for all children, but most of all for those who do not 'shape up' and therefore become aware that they disappoint. They begin to feel that love is dependent not upon who they are but upon what they can do, often with serious repercussions for their emotional well-being.

'**It's a tough world out there and only the fittest will survive. Jonathan is a bright boy and I want him to be top of the class.**
He should be reading better than he is by now or he'll be left behind.'
Ambitious father - MD of a local company

Sometimes expectations are wrong for the opposite reason but with equally serious consequences. A very able or gifted child can become frustrated and badly behaved because not enough is demanded of her/him. The educational programme may be insufficiently challenging and adult responses to the vast number of questions posed inadequate or non existent. Peers often find such children odd and exclude them socially. This only helps to exacerbate their problem. Help in identifying and catering for special needs of such children can be obtained from The National Association For Gifted Children (see back of book).

INCONSISTENCY

This may occur when two parents have a different approach to discipline, as in the following case study:
'Michael is very disruptive in the nursery. Other children do not want to play with him. When he approaches individuals or small groups he wrecks whatever they are doing. When they complain he usually responds by spitting, biting or hair pulling. We have to assign a member of staff to be near him all the time. We are

44

trying to work with his parents but this is not easy. Mum agrees that Michael can be difficult. He takes very little notice of her and she nags him in a quiet voice which rarely alters what he is doing. Then she gives up. Dad, on the other hand, is quite a different kettle of fish. Michael is afraid of him and does his bidding. Dad believes in strict discipline for boys, who he feels need a good hiding from time to time. He proudly boasts, "a good hiding never hurt me". Perhaps it is because he is so authoritarian that Mum gives in to Michael. She says he's too young (at four) to be expected to do as he's told all the time.'

Another feature of poor parenting is inconsistency in responses towards children's behaviour. If action A elicits a good telling off one day, but is ignored the next, or if action B is praised on one occasion, but receives no attention on another, a child could be forgiven for his confusion and might legitimately ask, 'so what is right and what is wrong?' It might even cause children to consciously or otherwise check again - perhaps by repeating bad behaviour just to find out! If bad actions are condemned consistently and good ones praised it soon becomes clear to a child how he can gain the praise he so dearly needs to build self-esteem. He will also learn how to avoid criticism, which is often a rather painful experience. In this way behaviour is moulded into an acceptable form.

Parental inconsistency can take another form which is equally confusing to a child, namely, when they say one thing while doing another. They may admonish a child for losing his temper while frequently doing so themselves, in which case it is not surprising if the child becomes rebellious. We have to remember that actions often speak louder than words!

Case study for inconsistency
Mr and Mrs Jarvison sat down together and decided what their daughter Annabelle should be expected to do in terms of behaviour.
She must always tell the truth
yet:
I know they told the Headteacher porkies when they said that they kept Annabelle away from school because she had a cold. They really went away for a long weekend.

She must not hurt other people
yet:
They sometimes slap their elder son when he does some misdemeanour or another.

She must share things with others
yet:
They tell the children to go to bed after a very plain tea. The children have seen the strawberries which their parents will eat as a dessert at the evening meal.

Persistent and petty nagging is also harmful, as it builds up a kind of immunity to what is requested by adults. Even worse is harsh discipline, affording little opportunity for the child to make free choices within a reasonable framework of rules, the reasons for which are carefully explained. Small children may respond to such a regime by becoming withdrawn. Conversely they may become rebellious and immune to successive stages in punishment. Shouting progresses to slapping, slapping becomes more severe until ultimately there is nowhere else to go and the child becomes immune to pretty well anything the parent says or does.

ROLE MODELS

Children pick up their codes of behaviour and moral values from those around them. If their parents or others close to them are aggressive, abusive, anti-authority, careless about their environment, or cruel in their dealings with other people, then it should not surprise us if their children follow suit. Such children have poor role models because of the example parents set.

Sometimes parents opt out of role modelling by default. This may be because they are either overworked and have no time or because they are depressed and unable to assume their role properly.
Rose is aged two. The childminder brings her to nursery every day. Rose's parents both work in London and are professional high fliers. Rose seems withdrawn and unhappy. She clings to nursery staff at the end of the day and clearly does not want to leave. Father is often abroad and mother has left a note on the child's file that she can only be disturbed in the most extreme emergencies as the meetings she leads are vital to the success of the company. She has left the childminder 'in charge' and she is the one who should be contacted.
The trouble is, the vacuum created by the absence of their influence has to be filled somehow, in the above case by the childminder. But too often it is filled by the vicarious influences of television or video. Not only are such influences often highly unsuitable, they do, in themselves, need careful discussion and explanation. Without an adult standing by, a young child finds it impossible to sort out fact from fantasy and may be frightened or disturbed by what he sees. The frequent

46

violence portrayed by television characters, even in children's programmes, is often acted out in the nursery or school playground as any childcare professional will testify.

In some cases it may be the insecurity of the parent which leads to the child's problem. They may wish to maintain the latter's state of dependency, inhibiting their development into separate human beings. In such cases they may try to hang on to them as long as possible, exaggerating any minor ailments as a justification for keeping them at home. All this makes it very difficult for the child to make or keep friends, face up to life's challenges or take the necessary steps to independence. Such children may be the subject of teasing by others for being a 'baby' and may even be bullied.

'Mrs P adores Charlie, as she calls him. She has been with him 24 hours a day for the last four years and found it difficult to bring him to nursery and then leave him with us. The health visitor has strongly advised her of the importance of giving Charlie more independence so he can get ready for school. He has very little experience of socialising and finds separation a painful experience. He cries hysterically when his mum goes and she is obviously very pained by the separation herself. She'll use any excuse to keep him away from nursery.'
Head of nursery

PHYSIOLOGICAL CAUSES

Some causes of worrying behaviour stem from a physiological rather than an emotional cause. Where this is the case, the child will obviously have special needs and require help and support from outside agencies. The nursery staff will have to work closely with parents and such agencies and agree a special programme of education for that particular child.

Although fairly rare, one of these conditions is hyperactivity. A truly hyperactive child is not to be confused with very lively children found at the end of the normal continuum. True hyperactivity is very difficult to deal with.

It is characterised by excessive physical and mental activity. Such children lack concentration, have short attention spans and are always 'on the go'. They often operate on a short fuse and are prone to frequent temper tantrums. To make matters worse for their parents and carers, they do not require much sleep and so are both trying and tiring to look after.

Genuinely hyperactive children require medical treatment. In some cases, most frequently in the United States and Australia, they are treated with drugs to calm them down.

Another disorder that nurseries may encounter is autism or its milder form, Aspergers syndrome. Here again, such children need specialist support. They do not form normal emotional attachments, have severe communication difficulties and normal speech development is impaired. Typically they manifest obsessive behaviour and repeat actions or insist on holding certain objects and carrying them around at all times. Hand flapping is another typical sign of autism.

Another disorder now identified is Attention Deficit Disorder (ADD). ADD is defined by Dr Green of the Royal Alexandra Hospital for Children in Sydney, Australia, as a cluster of behaviours such as inattention, poor impulse control, restlessness, disorganisation, poor self-motivation and inappropriate social skills.

The continuing identification of a variety of behaviour disorders underlines that nursery professionals need to keep their knowledge up-to-date through in-service training and professional publications.

DEATH AND SEPARATION

The death of a parent, grandparent, sibling or a family pet is a devastating event in the life of any child and will have inevitable consequences for his or her emotional well-being. Children react to such an event in different ways. They should, however, be allowed to express their grief through whatever means they choose. This may be through quietness, tears, or wishing to talk about it. Others may wish to paint pictures, act out the situation in role play or seek to identify characters in the same situation through stories and books.

'Melissa's Grandmother recently died of cancer. For some time prior to this sad death Melissa had been unhappy: her Grandma spent the last three weeks of her life in a Macmillan Hospice. A great air of sadness hangs over Melissa's family. She spends much of her time in nursery quietly playing with the dolls in the home corner or sitting on the settee in the book area. She has ceased to interact with the other children (before this situation arose Melissa was extremely outgoing). We give her as much one to one time as we can and listen sympathetically while she talks about her Grandma. We are always very sensitive when she paints pictures of her and then puts lots of black or dark brown colour in the background.

48

The feeling of loss experienced by Melissa is no doubt made worse by the fact that Grandma was a very loving primary carer who lived in the family home while mum worked.' Nursery key worker

Sometimes children may want to bring in a photograph of the deceased person, pet or something which had belonged to them. Nursery staff should respect such wishes, show an interest in them and talk things over with the child. They should at all costs resist the temptation to try to cheer the child up by saying such things as 'don't cry', 'dry those tears', 'cheer up' or seek to change the subject before the child is ready.

The separation and/or divorce of a child's parents inevitably seriously affects their emotional security. The close bond they have experienced with one parent is shattered and reactions to this vary again. Children may be withdrawn and find it difficult to concentrate or they may behave aggressively and destructively. Support should be provided not only to the child but also to the parent left with prime responsibility for care.

The situation is most damaging where the child is used as a pawn in bitter wranglings. Least harm will be done where both parents seek to reassure him of their love and try, at least in front of him, to co-operate over access. It is so much better if, for example, the parent with responsibility for care and maintenance allows the other to step over the threshold and perhaps have a cup of tea or coffee before taking the child out. The important influence of what the child experiences in relation to what is being said and what is being done is so obvious in the case of his parents. How can he be expected to imbibe into his moral framework the notion of care and kindness for others if he hears it said but experiences quite another reality.

'"We're going to move and my Daddy isn't coming with us. What will my Daddy do on his own? My Mummy says she never wants to see him again 'cause he's a horrible man." Giles (aged almost five). This devastating news was announced by Giles whose behaviour markedly changed from a sociable, hardworking little boy to one who is constantly attention seeking and unable to concentrate.'
Nursery nurse

There are other situations where separation from a parent may occur on a temporary basis, but still affect the child's ability to function effectively while he comes to terms with the changes. There may be times when a parent works abroad for a period, for example in the forces, or for a multinational company, where the parent works away during the week returning only at the weekends. The child might live with another parent/stepfamily at the weekend, returning to their 'base' family during the week. A parent, grandparent or sibling might enter hospital or be seriously ill at home, changing the family dynamics during the illness. All these life changes will inevitably affect children's behaviour in some way, and reassurance and empathy is the name of the game, keeping the known environment as safe and as familiar as possible.

In all cases of abnormal behaviour, parents and carers must also examine their own behaviour and ensure they are not negatively affecting the child's reaction to life. Children must also be helped to develop the language to enable them to express their feelings. This will be through role play, story, conversation, explanation, and creative outlets such as music, drama and art.

JEALOUSY

Here, we are talking about an emotional response to another person's perceived favoured position in family relationships. We are all very likely to have had feelings of jealousy at some time in our lives. It is a natural reaction to some changes in relationships, most notably for children with the arrival of a new sibling. It may also exist if parents do not succeed in treating both or all of their children fairly throughout their childhood.

'We first noticed something wrong when Lisa began to hit the dolls in the home corner and squeeze their arms ferociously - at the same time grimacing in such a way as to suggest the considerable force she was exerting. She also tore some of their clothes. We talked to her mother about this and together we came to the conclusion that feelings of jealousy were at the bottom of this behaviour. Mum confesses that she has been "very taken up with the new baby" and the situation has been made worse by the fact that the new baby was premature and therefore needed even more attention than a normal new-born.'
Nursery key worker

Jealousy is a manifestation of insecurity and unhappiness. To avoid its persistent negative effects adults need to recognise how children may be feeling. They should give them the attention they deserve and reassurance. In the case of a new arrival this is best done by careful preparation before a sibling's birth - including them in sharing information, decisions, practical preparations etc.
After the birth they should be included, wherever possible, in actual care, or parallel care with dolls. In addition 'special time' should be devoted exclusively to

the older child.

CHILD ABUSE

Children may be abused in several ways: emotionally, sexually, physically or through neglect. Sufferers will have varying ways of indicating their unhappiness. They are often anxious and may express this anxiety through aggression, being withdrawn, being tired, or projecting the experience suffered on to dolls, toys, pets or even other children.

In the case of physical abuse there will probably be signs such as bruising. Nurseries should discreetly seek an explanation from parents about any such signs and if they are not satisfied with the explanation put their child protection procedures into action. This will involve telling the parent(s) that they intend to inform the local social services and must be handled with great sensitivity.

CHAPTER NINE

Types of Bad Behaviour and How to Deal With Them

It is essential when addressing the wide spectrum of possible negative behaviours in children that professionals are aware and communicate to parents that certain behaviours at certain ages are acceptable, as part of the children's natural development. Other behaviours are out of the norm and make life difficult for the adults, but first and foremost for the children themselves. It is these behaviours that are labelled 'bad' or 'unacceptable' and need to be corrected to enable the children to develop socially and enjoy life.

The readers of Nursery World who responded to the survey 'Who's in control?' (22 August 1996) believe that children's behaviour has got worse over the past 10 years. The article 'A turn for the worse' (17 October 1996), based on nursery staff responses, listed the kind of behaviour causing parents most concern, such as temper tantrums.

The nursery staff found the most common difficulty they encountered was aggression, or more specifically, biting, disruption of activities, being destructive and then temper tantrums. The survey highlights a number of behaviours that exist and are unacceptable to our society. It is possible to list the most common types of behaviour that distract parents, nursery workers and children and then it is necessary to consider how to deal effectively with each one.

1. Temper tantrums.
2. Aggression - including fighting, biting, spitting, hitting, hair pulling.
3. Bullying, both physical and verbal.
4. Destructive behaviour - stopping others' creativity, breaking, throwing, demolishing.
5.Challenging authority - parents, staff, other adults, older children.
6. Anti social - unacceptable behaviour in terms of manners, swearing etc.
7. Withdrawn - unable to socialise.
8. Sexually unnatural behaviour.
9. Meal time disputes, picky eating.
10. The child with special educational needs.

Before we address each type of behaviour there are a number of 'ground rules' that are applicable to every behaviour and the way it is managed.

A. Every establishment needs to discuss and agree an effective behaviour policy (see Chapter 5).
B.This policy must be explained to the parents so that they can reinforce it at home, avoiding the children playing one group of adults off against another and providing the children with consistency.
C. It is the behaviour that must be labelled not the child.
D. Children must feel valued as individuals.
E. The emphasis should be on praising good behaviour and ignoring the bad behaviour as far as possible.
F. Use diversion away from the bad behaviour towards something different and positive.
G. Avoid shouting whenever possible.

TEMPER TANTRUMS

Temper tantrums are seen as part of growing up and of children establishing their place in the pecking order when they are about two years old. They become unacceptable when they continue to occur in three-, four- and five-year-olds.

53

However, whenever they occur they must be managed and the child helped to come to terms with the situation that sparked the tantrum off.

The adult must take control and stay calm - adding to the noise and discomfort of the situation by shouting yourself will not help. The child must be told calmly and clearly to stop shouting/kicking/crying so that the problem can be sorted out. Do not at this stage be tempted to bribe the child into quietness by a sweet/treat etc. Then the child needs to be told, ' when you are quiet we can talk/cuddle'. It is important to remember here that temper tantrums occur because the child feels out of control, possibly frightened and may be very tired. In the end they need to recognise your love for them and your calm control. It may be necessary to walk away from the child having its tantrum but keeping him/her in your sight saying, 'When you have calmed down, I'll come back and we can talk/cuddle'. As the child calms down - and they do eventually - make sure you then give him/her time to talk/cuddle, ask what it was about, explain the noise the tantrum had caused had upset you and maybe others, so try not to do it again. Leave them in no doubt that this behaviour is not acceptable but they are still loved. You may find they now need a rest or play with something quietly. This is because temper tantrums often leave children physically exhausted. While they are doing this you will also need to recover - what about a quiet cup of tea or a few deep breaths!

AGGRESSION

When one child attacks another through fighting, biting, spitting, hitting, hair pulling etc, he/she must be left in no doubt that this behaviour is not acceptable. A quick reaction to stop the behaviour by holding the perpetrator's hand and saying, 'No, we don't do that here', makes it very clear that the behaviour is disapproved of. What happens next very much depends upon the age of the children and the extent and frequency of the aggression.

Young children under two need the above step taken and the victim needs to be reassured and checked that they are not hurt. Indeed by giving attention to the victim rather than the perpetrator, we show that aggression does not gain our attention. Over two, it is necessary to start explaining to the aggressor in terms of, 'you would not like it if I did that to you'.

If a child above the age of three is aggressive towards another it may be necessary to follow up the initial reaction with a 'time out', telling them to sit on a chair for a few minutes (in your full view) to underline your deep dislike of the behaviour and then talk to them about how such behaviour hurts.

54

There is a debate about whether the perpetrator should be made to 'say sorry'. If you do take this line remember it must come from the child's understanding of what he/she has done is wrong, not just from your insistence that they parrot the words. You can put it another way by suggesting they make their victim feel better by giving them a hug.

BULLYING

Much has been written on this subject, particularly to do with older children, but it is important to recognise that both verbal and physical bullying is often a learned behaviour. It is important that the environment in which the children find themselves does not present bullying, in any form, as acceptable. This means that all adults must look at their own physical and verbal behaviour towards each other. They should be presenting a caring, supportive environment in which positive relationships are emphasised.

To counteract bullying, bullies and potential bullies must realise that their behaviour will be met with punishment. Underlying causes of bullying should of course, be investigated and dealt with. Victims and potential victims must realise that the adults will take them and their feelings seriously. If you do get a reported incident of bullying it is vital that you act quickly. Gather as much information as you can about the reported incident, decide whether bullying actually did occur and then speak to the accused child (you may have observed the incident yourself). Do this in a calm but firm manner, taking the child aside, and in turn listen to their explanation. Then explain to the bully why the actions are not acceptable and ask how would he/she feel if it had happened to them. End the conversation by giving the bully a clear positive message that you still like him/her, but explain what the penalty would be if it happens again. You must make sure that any penalty is carried out. Idle threats totally undermine your behaviour management system.

Efforts must be made to give the victim strategies to tackle the problems themselves by being more assertive.

It is useful to use situations such as role play and story time to emphasise co-operation and play down actions such as bullying.

DESTRUCTIVE BEHAVIOUR

Children who engage in this type of behaviour are usually angry about something

55

- either at themselves, something in their lives or at another person(s), so they damage items often without thinking why or of the results of their actions. It is important that the adults again intervene both physically and verbally in a calm manner to show the action and its consequences are not acceptable. Also, as in dealing with bullying, explain to the child that he/she would not like it if it happened to them. Then if it is appropriate ask the perpetrator to help the other child/ren to put things back to where they were or make other appropriate reparation. A moment of 'time out' may also be useful here.

CHALLENGING AUTHORITY

In these situations it is necessary to ask yourself if the authority you're upholding is realistic and practical, otherwise you will only get into a 'no win" situation. The authority you hold comes from sensible rules to ensure safety of the environment and from the respect you command from the children and other adults through your general demeanour and track record of how and why you implement the rules.

Although nursery age children do not fully understand rules, you help them to acquire an appreciation of their purpose by, for example, asking them what would happen under the following circumstances (and during the course of the actual activities):

   A. If when playing a board game one person moved the counter
     more than the dice indicated that they should.
   B. If at snack time the first person took all the biscuits or fruit for
   themselves.
   C. If in a game of 'Guess which instrument is playing' the blindfolded
   person peeped.

When children challenge authority it is necessary to say clearly and calmly:
'No, that is not possible because....................'.
'No, you know we don't do that because...................'.
'I am asking you to do this because..................'.
You will see from these statements it is necessary to take control but explain why you have made the decision. You must then ensure that your request is carried out. If the child fails to comply you may need to add a threat such as taking away some favourite activity, but make sure that any threat is carried through.

ANTI-SOCIAL BEHAVIOUR

This type of behaviour can only be prevented in an atmosphere where all adults concerned are clear about what is acceptable and what is expected in terms of social manners/behaviour so that the children can be presented with the correct model at all times. Then within this they can be told quietly, 'We don't do that or say that here'. It is important for staff to decide what social mores will be encouraged. It is essential that staff remember it is their responsibility to play their part in bringing up children who will find it easy to fit into society as a whole. Failure to do this impedes children's adjustment to life outside the nursery.

WITHDRAWAL

What should staff be doing to help the child who is withdrawn? This is perhaps even more serious than the overt unacceptable behaviour discussed above. It may be less annoying or less inconveniencing to staff, but a child displaying symptoms of withdrawal could well have deep seated emotional problems. Any such problems need to be discovered and solutions sought.

These children need their confidence to be built up by sympathetic staff who encourage them to enter into the variety of social gatherings. This could be by taking their hand and working alongside them so they have support and see how it is possible to engage in activities. Gradually the physical adult support can be withdrawn while verbal support and acclaim is continued until it becomes less necessary. The withdrawn child could be given time to act out possible fears in role play.

SEXUALLY UNNATURAL BEHAVIOUR

Children have to explore the roles of males and females in a variety of play situations. It is here that sometimes staff will see very explicit and perhaps uncomfortable (for them) play evolve.

It should be remembered, however, that strong biologically determined drives often prompt children to explore their own and each others' bodies. Such behaviour is natural and part of growing up. If the behaviour includes practices which children would not know about unless:

      A. They had seen them on TV/video,
      B. They had seem adults in action.

C. Adults have involved them in an abusing situation.

Then it will be necessary to take prompt action by talking to parents and, if necessary, social services.

In whatever way you may need to intervene in such play, it must be done sensitively, have due regard to children's feelings at the time. It could also be harmful for their future psychological well-being in relation to sexual matters if undue attention is drawn to them, with possible resultant feelings of guilt.

MEAL TIME DISPUTES, PICKY EATING

This is an area that often concerns parents and by the time they speak to staff at a nursery, meal times may have become a battle of wills. In the nursery, staff have a much easier job, as any difficulties with food are not so personalised and the presence of other children who enjoy meal times and a variety of food are a great incentive. It is important that meal times should be presented as a relaxed, enjoyable part of the day where the emphasis is not on the food so much as the social meeting and sharing of the meal. Children should be given some choice as to what is put on their plate and only small portions given at any one time. As this is eaten, a gentle congratulations for clearing their plate or comment such as, 'that was nice wasn't it?', should follow and then the child should be asked if they want any more. Their favourite food can always be held as a reward for eating something they are not used to. If a child has asked for a certain food they should be encouraged to finish this. Stopping children picking between meals will also help them as they will be more ready to eat at the required time. Do not force a child to eat what he/she really does not like - we all have our preferences and some foods do honestly make us feel sick!

SPECIAL EDUCATIONAL NEEDS

A child with special educational needs should not be seen as one who automatically presents bad behaviour. But their condition may mean their behaviour is not as acceptable as that of the majority of children and so careful consideration of how these children are supported must be part of their programme.

To achieve a stepped programme of support as presented in the five stages of the Code of Practice (DFEE 1994) observation must come first as may also be necessary for other children presenting difficult behaviour. Only through systematic observation can staff assess what it is that affects a child's behaviour. Analysis of recorded observations should enable staff to put into place a programme of remediation.

Perhaps every person working with children should here remember the maxim:
> IF A CHILD
> If a child lives with criticism he learns to condemn
> If a child lives with ridicule he learns to be shy
> If a child lives with tolerance he learns to be patient
> If a child lives with encouragement he learns to have confidence
> If a child lives with fairness he learns justice
> If a child lives with approval he learns to know himself
> If a child lives with love around him he learns to bring love into the world

Remember, it is the behaviour we do not like, not the child.

CHAPTER TEN

Strategies to be Used in Very Difficult Cases

With children whose behaviour is persistently difficult and causing real concern, you will need to:

1. Assign him/her much closer adult supervision.

2. Give very clear instructions about what he/she is to do for the next session.

3. Divide the day up into short time spans with clear expectations of what the child is to do - both your choice and his.

4. Give clear explanations of the rules surrounding each activity, for example, 'We don't throw sand. We don't take tools from other children.'

5. Gently but firmly hold child's hands and demand eye contact while you speak. Ensure the child has understood what you are saying. Perhaps repeat on completion your oral instructions.

6. Split activity goals into small units - the more difficult the child the smaller the units need to be.

7. This makes it easier to get an element of achievement. It is through such elements of achievement, no matter how small, that praise can begin. 'Well done' stickers or pendants with the words 'I'm a good boy/girl' are often helpful in changing a child's view of self.

60

Indeed, believing that you're naughty may actually cause you to conform to the label and vice versa.

8. The child is now in the first stages of being 'good' and 'doing the right thing'. It can be pointed out that when he/she has collected N symbols of praise then they can have a reward - something of their own choice, something to strive for.

9. Having a collection of 'tokens of acclaim' which can be added to gives the opportunity for a public praise at circle time. 'Look everybody, X has been a good boy again and he has another sticker.' In such cases the child enjoys the acclaim and, importantly, other children will begin to change their perception of him.

10. Tokens can, of course, be taken away! But at least you now have some leverage on behaviour.

11. Very gradually, the rigid timetabling and vigilant overseeing should be able to be relaxed.

12. Gaining co-operation. Co-operation with others is a social skill which very difficult children find hard. Under the closest supervision and with the choice of the most suitable partner, increasing time should be spent learning how to co-operate.

Exercises involving co-operation include:

1. Rowing the boat - face to face sitting exercise holding hands and bending backwards and forwards as if rowing.
2. Making each other a drink - lemon squash/orange squash, asking, 'how would you like me to make it for you?' Then enjoying drinking it. Washing up cups afterwards.
3. Helping a blind-folded partner find locations within the nursery.
4. Playing a simple board game for two.

OBSERVING AND RECORDING DIFFICULT BEHAVIOUR

If a child's behaviour is causing you concern, in order to set about devising an effective programme of support you will first need to systematically record and date your observations, which can then be shared with parents and staff.

Here is a case study of a child called Janice. She is aged three years and two months. Her key worker has recorded incidents of her aggressive behaviour, and added her comments and plans for action as she follows each incident.

Staff in a nursery may wish to use this as a model.
Observation 8 January 19..

Janice came in a tearful mood today. When I presented her with the water play bowl and various plastic containers (she usually delights in water play) she did not display her usual enthusiasm. After approximately five minutes during which time she filled the bottles then let the water splash back into the bowl she wanted a cuddle on my lap. 'Cuddle, cuddle,' she said. I asked her if she would like me to read her a story. 'Mme' she replied, which is her way of saying yes. I carried her over to the story box, picked out *Where is Spot* and began reading to her. Then Thomas (aged three), who had been playing with the garage set, made as if to climb on to my lap as well.

Janice was very resentful and demonstrated this by kicking him away and shouting 'no, no'. When he tried to push past her kicking feet she tried to reach out and scratch his face.

I told her that we all loved her but we did not like it when she hurt other people. 'We must be kind', I said 'and stop trying to hurt poor Thomas.' She carried on half crying and half screaming and it took me about ten minutes to calm her. Finally I managed to distract her with the farm box.

Comment

Janice is clearly very unhappy. Tears have not been far away all day. Her difficulty in sharing with other children continues.

Action

Try to raise her self-esteem with lots of appropriate responsibility and praise. I shall try to foster a nurturing attitude with dolls and toys and comment positively when she seems to care for them. I'll gradually try to include Thomas.

Observation 15 January

I set up a cooking activity. Janice really enjoys cooking and I felt it would be a good way of getting her playing with Thomas. I let them take turns to rub in the mixture, based strictly on fair timing (I used the sand egg timer). At first Janice seemed to be coping well and I praised her profusely. Trouble began when I asked her to add half the jug full of milk to the mixture. She refused to hand over to Thomas for him to take his turn with pouring. She grabbed the bowl to herself and pulled Thomas' hair. After reminding her that we must all try to be kind to one another and that she must have hurt poor Thomas she said, 'I hate you, I hate you - you bastard'. She threw the entire mixture on the floor and burst into tears.

Comment

We were just beginning to have some success when she snapped. I am concerned about her violent action and language. Where is she learning this behaviour from? Why is she so unhappy?

Action

I feel I must continue with the praise and play programme described in the action plan above. I will also talk to her parents, though they are not the easiest of people to communicate with, and see if I can glean anything about the situation at home. If things don't improve I'll seek help from the health visitor.

Observation 20 January

Janice was sitting on the carpet with her dolls. She was putting them into bed and covering them up with the blankets I had specially made for the doll play. She made crying noises (for the dolls) and then shouted, 'Shut up, shut up and go to sleep when you're told'. She made more crying noises and shouted the same words again, adding, 'I'm coming upstairs to you'. She took the dolls from the bed roughly by the elbows and shook them violently before taking off her shoe and hitting them on the bottom.

Comment

This violent behaviour enacted against the dolls is very worrying. I feel I will have to speak to someone and seek advice.

The outburst of temper has a dramatic element, with the dolls being punished physically for not going to bed and to sleep as requested.

Action

I will do some imaginative play with Janice, involving the dolls. I will model kindness towards them and encourage her to do the same. I will provide her with the necessary resources to play at nurturing and will praise her for any acts of kindness I observe.

I wonder if this violence is a way for her to play out her feelings? - perhaps I should ignore the rough stuff and just praise the good.

Observation 28 January

Today I noticed some bruising on Janice. Her left arm has what looks like purple X-ray fingers. She has been rather quiet and withdrawn all day while with me.

When her father came to pick her up he asked me if I had had any trouble with her.

'No', I replied, 'Today has been a rather quiet day. But to tell you the truth I am concerned about Janice and the outbursts of temper and aggression which she displays from time to time'.

'She can be a real little bitch at times,' he said. 'She needs to learn that she can't always have her own way.'

I tried to tell him that pre-school children do like to have their own way and do sometimes have difficulty in controlling their feelings. I went on to explain that gradually learning how to behave satisfactorily with other people does develop and it's really a matter of keeping calm and patient and showing by our own behaviour, how it's done.

We both helped Janice to put on her coat, then she suddenly rushed into the toilet and slammed the door. She held on to the door with considerable force and was screaming. Finally, I managed to open the door and remove her hands from it. Mr X flushed, grabbed her by the elbow and smacked her so hard on the bottom that she was flung against the basin. 'That will teach you to play around when I've got to go to work,' he said.

Comment

My suspicions have been confirmed. Mr X treats Janice very harshly and the violence of his reaction and the severity of the smack were out of all proportion. I shall have to report it.

Action

It is essential we provide Janice with a continuingly calm, supportive and loving environment at the nursery including activities where she will succeed, boosting her self-esteem.

CHAPTER ELEVEN

Personal And Social Development - Ideas For Meeting The Criteria

In conclusion we have written this chapter on children's personal and social development. We have taken the 13 criteria identified by the Schools Curriculum and Assessment Authority and suggested ways in which they may be achieved. SCAA has placed this area of learning at the head of the three most important. It is the foundation without which any other successful learning is unlikely to take place. It is about being able to take advantage of one's education and being a happy and fulfilled human being.

This area of learning is very much concerned with good behaviour through promoting children's emotional well-being and ability to enjoy successful social relationships, developing independence and the cultural, spiritual and moral dimensions of their character.

CRITERION 1 - HAVE CONFIDENCE AND SELF RESPECT

• Design the individual's learning programme so that it embodies challenge yet is achievable.

•Discuss a child's achievements with him or her directly and in front of peers and parents with the child present.

•Display work. Where this is not of a permanent nature, as in block constructions for example, photograph the child beside it.

•Listen attentively to what the child says and make reference to it in later encounters - thus demonstrating real interest.

•Sometimes provide a running commentary on what the child is doing - this says you're interested and helps with language development.

•Ask for the child's opinion and ideas.

•Ask the child to help you or others.

•Celebrate individuals' birthdays.

•Supply tokens of acclaim judiciously - e.g. stickers and stars.

CRITERION 2 - BEHAVE IN APPROPRIATE WAYS

•Make sure children know and understand the nursery's code of behaviour (Behaviour Policy).

•Uphold your policy fairly and consistently - have your parents 'on board'.

•Praise good behaviour.

•Be good role models.

•Discuss right and wrong in appropriate contexts as they arise in the nursery.

•Avoid trouble by being well organised - don't let children be bored, plan effectively and get your groupings right.

•Recognise the value of role play in helping children to encounter problem situations which require them to find their own solutions - only step in if you must.

•Give reasons for your judgments where conflict occurs.

•Where bad behaviour exists explain why it cannot be tolerated - speak quietly, slowly and firmly and insist that the child gives you eye contact.

•Encourage children to understand the consequences of their actions.

CRITERION 3 - BE AWARE OF RIGHT AND WRONG

This concept develops slowly throughout childhood. The famous developmental psychologist Jean Piaget conducted an experiment on children's moral understanding. It consisted of telling stories and asking children to say which characters were the naughtiest. The experiment revealed that up to the age of nine or ten children tend to see the degree of naughtiness in terms of consequences rather than the intentions of the perpetrator. Thus a child who accidentally broke 15 cups was seen (by a six year old) as deserving more severe punishment than another who was engaged in (illicitly) taking jam while his mother was out and breaking one cup in the process.

Our role in helping children understand right and wrong is helped by:-

    •The wise use of literature, TV etc.
    •Discussions.
    •Being very positive when right is done and condemning wrong actions
    - *not* the children who do them.

CRITERION 4 - WORK WELL IN GROUPS AND ARE WILLING TO TAKE TURNS AND SHARE FAIRLY

•Have appropriate group size and composition when planning activities. Some children work well together while others don't.

•Play games involving turn taking from those featuring board and dice to simple team games with small apparatus outside.

•Make sure that 'prestigious' items like bikes and computers are shared fairly. Name lists to be ticked should ensure that everyone who wants to has a go. Timers are useful to ensure fairness.

•Products of cooking activities, snacks etc should be seen to be shared fairly at circle time. Adults should make reference to the importance of fairness when cutting fruit or cakes.

•Plan activities which require, for a successful outcome, that children do co-operate, eg painting a large model, ring games, making music.

•Have resources which demand co-operation, eg large wheeled vehicles, group block play, ball games.

•Again, remember the value of the home corner in throwing up situations where co-operation is essential.

CRITERION 5 - TREAT LIVING THINGS, PROPERTY AND THEIR ENVIRONMENT WITH CARE AND CONCERN

•Make sure that living things (plants and animals) do feature in your establishment. Animals need not be long term residents - mini beasts, fish, wild birds in the nursery garden are not arduous to keep.

•Make sure that any animals (living things which are not plants) are kept and housed in a manner which conforms to health and safety requirements.

•Emphasise the responsibility we have in looking after animals and their dependency upon us for their welfare.

• Talk about the need to provide living conditions which match, as closely as possible, the creature's natural environment.

• Provide places where individuals can store their own property.

• Insist on a, 'borrow it, use it and return it', regime in relation to reusable items of equipment.

• Insist on children using space responsibly eg, preparing tables for painting, tidying up after themselves.

• Take children on walks round the locality and point out evidence of care within it as well as interesting natural phenomena.

• Have nursery collections of suitable materials for recycling.

• Encourage responsible use of the waste paper bin.

• Use designated parts of the nursery garden for cultivation.

CRITERION 6 - HAVE GOOD RELATIONSHIPS WITH AND SENSITIVITY TO OTHERS, INCLUDING THOSE OF DIFFERENT CULTURES AND BELIEFS

• Good role modelling by staff caring for children, including the way they interact with children's parents.

• Encourage co-operation through planned activities.

• Make reference to the needs and feelings of others in discussions.

• Praise acts of kindness displayed by children.

• Plan for the satisfaction of children's natural nurturing instinct by including caring activities in your role play programme.

• Encourage children to be sympathetic to those who may have hurt themselves or be upset.

• Stimulate problem solving activities which involve making or doing things which meet other people's needs.

• Invite people from other cultures into nursery to 'show and tell' features of their way of life.

• Create whole or part displays which relate to the lives of those from other cultures.

• Correct any unpleasant remarks made about other people. (This should include the stereotypic sentiments expressed by elements in the media about some of our European partners which can be picked up by children).

• Provide resources, including artefacts, dolls, books, music, dressing up clothes and pictures from other cultures.

• Possibly celebrate a variety of religious and other festivals.

• Point out any features in the locality related to other groups, eg places of worship, restaurants or shops.

• Modify the home corner sometimes so that items within it reflect cultural diversity.

• Prepare dishes from other cultures.

• Make sure that all children - boys and girls, those with special needs - have equal access to what the nursery offers. It is important that they also share responsibilities as well as rights!

CRITERION 7 - SHOW A RANGE OF FEELINGS SUCH AS WONDER, JOY OR SORROW

• Stimulate curiosity with items from the natural and man made world, including simple mechanisms.

• Encourage detailed observation of natural phenomena.

•Include plenty of opportunities to celebrate within your programme.

•Present a variety of music to match mood.

•Plan activities which stimulate all of the senses.

•Take children into the wider world - there is so much to wonder at and enjoy, make sure experiences are coupled with good quality explanation and discussion.

•Recognise that sad things happen. Enable children to express their grief - it does not help to deny.

•Encourage children's attention to the fate of those in stories or on film through sensitive discussion.

•When tragic things happen like the death or severe illness in a child's family, allow for the open expression of individual grief.

•Have books within your collection with which children in difficult situations can identify.

•Provide means of expression through plenty of creative work.

•Encourage children to comfort others through making and doing things, eg 'get well' cards.

CRITERION 8 - RESPOND TO CULTURAL AND RELIGIOUS EVENTS

•Celebrate appropriately - make decorative items, cook and enjoy the food, dress up, carry out appropriate aspects of ritual.

•Have or simulate the necessary artefacts to make all this possible.

•Make sure that you are knowledgeable.

•Present appropriate literature.

•Invite representatives from other cultural/religious groups.

CRITERION 9 - CONCENTRATE AND PERSEVERE

•Congratulate children on the completion of tasks.

•Site activities appropriately in relation to one another to avoid unnecessary noise and disturbance.

•Make sure you avoid frustration or interruptions to concentration by having sufficient resources for an activity.

•Intervene when frustration threatens.

•Give sufficient time for children to really 'settle down'.

•Any items which are incomplete should be carefully preserved if at all possible, for completion later.

•Encourage parents to value their child's work.

•For some children you will need to stage goals within a task to give them a sense of satisfaction along the way.

•Get group size and composition right.

•It is helpful to define the territory of an activity by, for example, having a special mat upon which others should not encroach!

•Make sure activities are worthwhile and achievable.

•Build new skills etc on a foundation of experience.

•Praise and value what has been achieved by displays, for example, or presentations at circle time.

CRITERION 10 - TAKE INITIATIVE

•Provide adequate time for children to make their own choices with regard to the activities they wish to pursue.

•Let them choose who they work with sometimes.

•Don't let adults over-control the nursery programme or be too bound by timetables and routines.

•Within an adult-led activity, respond to individual children's suggestions and ideas.

CRITERION 11 - ABLE TO SELECT AN ACTIVITY OR RESOURCES

•Within the constraints of health and safety considerations, make resources available for children to choose and select freely.

•Encourage children to plan their own programme for part of the time. It is a good idea to get them to verbalise this plan and follow it up at the end of the session with discussion - 'how did it go?' Perhaps the child has something to show?

•Resources should be stored in such a manner that they are easily accessible.

•They should be at the right height and easy to take.

•It should be clear what storage boxes contain - to meet the needs of all stages of development you could label with an actual item from the box, a picture of it and the printed word.

•Wherever possible use see-through storage.

•It should be made clear where children should return items so that others can then use them - silhouettes of their shape to indicate where they belong can be useful in this regard.

•There should be enough resources to satisfy reasonable demand - keep an eye out for shortages or replacement need.

•Make sure you have sufficient 'basic provision' to encourage worthwhile choice.

CRITERION 12 - WORK WELL INDEPENDENTLY

•Give individuals sufficient space to carry out their work. Again a 'territory marker' in the form of a mat may be useful to enable an individual to pursue some activities.

•Be responsive to children's own plans and ideas - aim to facilitate rather than block.

•Congratulate independent efforts.

CRITERION 13 - HAVE PERSONAL INDEPENDENCE

•Have resources which enable children to practice with various fastening systems like lacing and buttons.

•Give children plenty of time to dress themselves for outdoor activities/going home - congratulate successes.

•Have routines for hand washing, tooth cleaning etc so that children come to regard such practices as part of everyday living.

•Have the right kind of protective aprons which are easy to access, put on and return.

•Provide necessary storage for clothing/shoes and personal belongings.

References

[1] The survey 'Who's In Control in Your Nursery' appeared in the 22 August 1996 issue of *Nursery World*

[2] *The Independent,* article by Andreas Whittam Smith ' A Government Policy Stolen From King Canute' 2/12/96

[3] Reported in *The Independent* 25/8/96, research published Sept '96 by Dr Arlene Vetere et al Reading University

[4] *Sunday Times* article 'Give Children Time Not Television' 2/6/96

[5] Article from *The Observer* by Barry Hugill 8/8/93. 'The Horror Of Being A Child In The Nineties'. Findings from Policy Studies Institute Think Tank Study

[6] Article 'The Loss Of Our Innocence' *The Independent* 15/8/96

[7] Lefkowitz MM et al 'Growing Up To Be Violent' New York and Oxford Pergamon

Bibliography

Children's Developmental Progress From Birth To Five Years
Sheridan M (1973)   Windsor: NFER

Closely Observed Children
M Armstrong (1980)   London: Writers & Readers

Code of Practice On The Identification and Assessment of Special Educational Needs
DFEE   ISBN 0855 22 444 4

Control and Discipline In Schools
Docking JW (1980)   London: Harper & Row

Early Childhood Development and Education
Donaldson M, Grieve R, Pratt C (Eds) (1983)   Oxford: Blackwell

Educating Young Children
Mary Hohmann and David P Weikart, High/Scope Educational Research Foundation(1995)   Highscope Press Ypsilanti Michigan

Early Childhood Education: A Developmental Curriculum
Blenkin GM and Kelly AV (Eds) (1987)   London: Paul Chapman

Family Change and Future Policy
Family Policy Studies Centre   London: Joseph Rowntree Trust

77

Playing It Safe
Diana McNeish and Dr Helen Roberts   Barnardos: tel 0181 550 8822

Pre-School Provision For Children With Special Needs
Robson B (1989)   London: Casselll

The Children We Deserve
Dr Rosalind Miles (1995)   Harper Collins

Willstaar Manual (related to speech and language)
Willstaar Ltd, PO Box 176 Macclesfield, Cheshire SK10 55W

Working Towards Partnership in the Early Years
Pugh G and De'Ath E (1989)   National Children's Bureau

Useful Contacts

Barnardos
Tel 0181 550 8822

Forum On Children and Violence
Contact Janet Convery, The National Children's Bureau, Tel 0171 843 6309

National Association For Gifted Children
Tel 01908 673677

Parents Groups
Parent line, tel 01702 554782
Parent Link, tel 0171 735 1214
For single parents: SPAN, tel 0117 951 4231, SPHERE, tel 01734 591604

Reading Children's Information Centre
(Thames Valley only) Tel 01734 509499

NOTES

NOTES